LeBron James
In His Own Words

LeBron James
In His Own Words
Young Reader Edition

EDITED BY
**Elizabeth Pappas
and Emily Feng**

A B2 BOOK

AGATE

CHICAGO

ISBN-13: 978-1-57284-339-4
ISBN-10: 1-57284-339-X
eISBN-13: 978-1-57284-887-0
eISBN-10: 1-57284-887-1

Printed in the United States of America

The Library of Congress has cataloged the earlier edition of this book as follows:

Names: Pappas, Elizabeth, editor. | Feng, Emily, editor.
Title: LeBron James in his own words / Edited by Elizabeth Pappas and Emily Feng.
Description: Chicago : Agate Publishing, Inc., [2023] | Series: In their own words
Identifiers: LCCN 2023032453 (print) | LCCN 2023032454 (ebook) | ISBN 9781572843288 (paperback) | ISBN 9781572848818 (epub)
Subjects: LCSH: James, LeBron. | African American basketball players--Biography. | Basketball players--United States--Biography. | Political activists--United States--Biography. | African American philanthropists--Biography.
Classification: LCC GV884.J36 L38 2023 (print) | LCC GV884.J36 (ebook) | DDC 796.323092 [B]--dc23/eng/20230719
LC record available at https://lccn.loc.gov/2023032453
LC ebook record available at https://lccn.loc.gov/2023032454

10 9 8 7 6 5 4 3 2 1   24 25 26 27 28 29

B2 is an imprint of Agate Publishing. Agate books are available in bulk at discount prices. For more information, go to agatepublishing.com.

I think legacy will speak for itself. Who I am as a man and what I do off the floor defines my legacy more than what I do on the court.

—LEBRON JAMES

Contents

Introduction

Few people have been burdened with the expectations placed on a teenage LeBron James at the outset of his professional basketball career. Even fewer have exceeded them.

Drafted first overall at eighteen, he's since won four NBA championships, earned four MVP awards and two Olympic gold medals, and been selected for nineteen All-Star teams. While he's become the all-time leading scorer in the NBA, he also ranks fourth in career assists, and he's famed for his devotion to team play.

But it's James's achievements off the court, from activism to business success, that truly set him apart as a cultural force. What it all comes back to, what's clearly his core motivation, is inspiring youth.

His own childhood was difficult. James's mother, Gloria, struggled to provide for him on her own, and they moved from place to place in the rougher areas of Akron, Ohio. James is devoted to his mother, who was loving and supportive even as she struggled to find steady work. When James was nine, his mother made a painful sacrifice, sending him to live with his football coach Frank Walker's family so that he could have a more stable home environment. James went from missing nearly as much school as he attended one year to winning the perfect attendance award the next.

The Walkers did more than help set James on the right path. They also handed him a basketball. Although he had started out playing football, James quickly became a basketball sensation. Not only was he breaking records left and right, but by the end of his high school career his games were selling out 9,000-seat arenas, with tickets reselling for $2,000. NBA scouts were calling him the "greatest player [they'd] ever seen." *Sports Illustrated* described him as "the Chosen One." Just before the NBA draft, he signed an $87 million deal with Nike; in fact, James had been on the Nike talent scouts' radar since he was in the eighth grade.

It was a lot to live up to. James started off strong. Right out of high school, his hometown Cleveland Cavaliers made him the first overall pick in the 2003 NBA draft. James was named Rookie of the Year, then was named an All-Star for the first time his second year. For those first two seasons, however, Cleveland missed the playoffs. Although James continued amassing personal success, he couldn't carry the Cavaliers to a championship during his initial run with his hometown team.

Enter *The Decision*. In a sixty-minute ESPN live special, James announced his move to the Miami Heat, where he formed a "super team" with fellow stars Dwyane Wade and Chris Bosh. The ill-considered special made James a villain to millions overnight. There was immense criticism about the spectacle; some felt it was narcissistic, while many more saw it as an affront to the Ohio fans who'd supported him since he was a teen. Some even burned his jerseys. However, James's remarkable ability to recover from missteps like *The Decision* is a key part of his greater significance.

During his four seasons in Miami, James eventually won two NBA championships and was twice named the NBA Finals MVP. His role in using his free agency to help form a team where he could have such success ushered in a new era of player empowerment; James helped shift the entire power dynamic between the league and its star players. James's appeal has been so great that he's even reshaped traditional fandom, with many now considering themselves "LeBron fans" instead of fans of any one team.

After finding success in Miami, James made the less controversial decision to return to Cleveland. Winning as many championships as he could for himself wasn't enough—he wanted to bring a title to his hometown, too. And he did: in his second season back, James led his team to a win that ended a fifty-two-year championship drought.

After James moved once again to join the Los Angeles Lakers, he experienced the first significant injury of his career in his first season, missing the playoffs for the first time since 2005. The following year, in the 2019–2020 season, James was back, and the Lakers won James's fourth title from within the NBA's pandemic "bubble." Once again, James was named Finals MVP.

James has earned additional recognition for his success off the court. According to *Forbes*, James became a billionaire around 2022, the first active NBA player ever to do so (Michael Jordan hit the milestone after retirement). James is an astute businessman, owning SpringHill, a production company, and investing in numerous other enterprises. By relying not just on traditional endorsements but also partnerships and ownership/investments, James spearheaded a new form of sports marketing that afforded him another type of empowerment.

And James certainly makes that money work. Success on the court isn't just about the game, or the money in his pocket. It's about showing kids what they can do. Beyond providing a living example and making substantial donations to various charities, James created his own charity, the LeBron James Family Foundation, to strengthen community and help families and children in Akron. Through the foundation, he created the I PROMISE School, providing education, food, and transportation to school for kids, and even GEDs and job help for parents, with a mission to support the most at-risk students.

James prioritizes inspiring his own children, too. He is clearly—and publicly—an involved father to his three children, cheering courtside at basketball games for his two sons and making cooking videos for YouTube with his daughter.

Since rising to superstardom, James has always spoken up for what he believes in, including advocating for the Black Lives Matter movement. James launched More Than a Vote, a campaign to empower Black voters and combat voter suppression, during the NBA All-Star game in 2020, using his visibility as an athlete to speak up for what's really important.

Part I

EARLY LIFE

Growing Up

MAN, I'M JUST a kid from Akron, Ohio. Wow, I'm truly blessed.

—**Twitter, December 22, 2011**

EDITORIAL NOTE: Akron, Ohio, is a city forty miles south of Cleveland. It has a population of just under 200,000 people.

I WOULDN'T BE here today without my mom; she's like my best friend. Just knowing the sacrifices she, you know, had and did and everything was like for me. My mom was sixteen years old when she had me, and as a kid you don't really understand that. When you get older and you have kids of your own you're like, "Oh my god, you was a high school sophomore?!" Just knowing the commitment that she had for me and the sacrifice: there's nothing in this world I wouldn't do for her. I am who I am because of her.

—**NBA on TNT, February 19, 2023**

WHEN I WAS five, some financial things happened, and I moved seven times in a year. We moved from apartment to apartment, sometimes living with friends. My mom would always say, "Don't get comfortable, because we may not be here long."

—ESPN, December 23, 2002

IN FOURTH GRADE, I missed 82 days of school. Out of 160.

—ESPN, December 23, 2002

I NEVER COMPLAINED. Never. We were already going through tough times. It doesn't make it any better if I'm complaining. My mother said it was time to go, I packed my little book bag and it was time to roll.

I remember my mother sitting me down and basically telling me because of certain situations, that she may be gone for a little while, that I was going to be living with one of my coaches. It was a challenge. That's all I cared about when I was growing up—if I was gonna be able to wake up and my mother was still alive or still by my side. That was—because I was already without a father, you know, and I didn't want to be without both of my parents so it was definitely scary and tough.

—*More Than a Game*, September 6, 2008

MY LIFE CHANGED. I had shelter and food.

—on moving in with coach Frankie Walker and family,
ESPN, December 23, 2002

[FIFTH GRADE] I played little league football for the first time, and in the six games I scored eighteen touchdowns and we won the city championship. And at that point I was like, "This is something I want to do." I loved the concept of [a] team.

—*Road Trippin'* **podcast, March 2017**

THE THING THAT I had on the court that I didn't have off the court was security. Because every day we went to the gym, I knew I was gonna get picked, we were gonna win basketball games or we were gonna win pickup games. I've always said it's home away from home for me.

—*More Than a Game*, **September 6, 2008**

I GREW UP in Akron, and there was no LeBron James to look up to.... You grow up in Chicago, you got Walter Payton, Michael Jordan. You grow up in Akron, you got Goodyear!

—*Esquire*, October 2008

EDITORIAL NOTE: Walter Payton was a record-breaking football player who played for the Chicago Bears for 13 seasons. Michael Jordan is one of the greatest basketball players of all time, winning six championships with the Chicago Bulls. The Goodyear tire company was founded in Akron in 1898 and is still based there today.

WHAT HELPED ME in school was sports. When I was eight, nine, that was the first time I started playing organized sports and I had coaches around me that stressed education and not being allowed to play if we weren't doing our schoolwork or being at school on time, things like that.

—ESPN, July 6, 2011

THEY SAID, "YOU are an inner-city kid, you are **underprivileged**, you live in poverty, you are not going to make it out." I mean, I would have lost a long time ago if I would have listened to what the narration of it all is.

—*Kneading Dough: The Podcast,* **March 5, 2019**

UNDERPRIVILEGED (adj.): not provided the same social or economic rights as other members of a society

High School

HIGH SCHOOL FOR me is the best time of my life.

—*Road Trippin'* podcast, December 2017

IF YOU WERE an inner-city kid, you went to Buchtel. It was definitely an all-Black school so everybody expected us to be there. . . . Choosing to go to St. V was definitely bigger than just picking one high school over another. People look at you like you were choosing race.

—*More Than a Game*, September 6, 2008

EDITORIAL NOTE: Buchtel Community Learning Center is a public middle and high school in Akron at which roughly 90 percent of the student population is Black. At St. Vincent–St. Mary High School, the private Catholic school in Akron that James attended, the student population is 22 percent Black.

THAT EIGHTEEN-YEAR-OLD KID was just super excited to just start his journey, and I didn't know what to expect but I knew I belonged and I knew I could play in this league with the big boys.

—ESPN, February 8, 2023

GOING INTO SENIOR season, I started thinking "How am I gonna set our team up the right way to win it next year?" It was an eye-opener for me. On me being a leader that I wanted to be for our team.

—More Than a Game, **September 6, 2008**

WE WON BECAUSE we were together. We won because we respected Coach Dru as a coach, as a mentor, as a leader, and we had one goal and that was to win a national championship. And we wouldn't let nothing stand in our way.

—More Than a Game, **September 6, 2008**

> EDITORIAL NOTE: Coach Dru Joyce II began coaching James when he was ten years old and coached him through his entire basketball career at St. Vincent–St. Mary High School.

MY GAMES GOT moved from our high school to the university, and our games started being televised. People would be out on the streets selling T-shirts with my **likeness** on it. I'm a pretty smart guy. And I wasn't getting none of it, and my mom wasn't getting none of it.

—*Shut Up and Dribble*, November 3, 2018

LIKENESS (noun): picture of a person

I GO FROM $10 in my pocket to $100 million. In high school. Yup.

—*GQ*, February 18th, 2014

I WAS ON the cover of *Sports Illustrated* when
I was in the eleventh grade, and I just thought
I was doing another cover of another sports
magazine. I didn't know how big it was at the
time. I didn't know till I was like twenty-one
years old how big *Sports Illustrated* was, and then
I was like, Wow! I was pretty big in high school!

—*Esquire*, **October 2008**

MY WHOLE CAREER has been built off trial and
error. I ain't have nobody when I came in at 18
[who] had an open-door policy for me, to help
guide me through what I was about to go into. So
it's been trial and error . . . just being a sponge.

—*Sports Illustrated*, **August 30, 2022**

> **EDITORIAL NOTE:** An open-door policy refers to a rule at an
> organization where members or employees can easily talk to
> someone more senior than themselves to discuss questions or
> concerns.

PEOPLE ASK ME if it's a hard decision going to the NBA, but I've made harder decisions. Decisions about smoking or going to school, or stealing from a store or not stealing. Those are harder decisions.

—**ESPN, December 23, 2002**

BEING A **first-generation** money-maker in the household is a scary thing. For an eighteen-year-old, I go from sitting in classrooms in May ... to being a multimillionaire a month later in June, which is insane. It's hard to kind of process that. It's a scary thing.

—*Kneading Dough: The Podcast*, **March 5, 2019**

FIRST-GENERATION (adj.): the first member of a family to reach a certain milestone

AT EIGHTEEN YEARS old I knew I had to play the game, I knew I belonged in the NBA, but I didn't know what I could become at eighteen. I just knew that if I continue to put in the work and I continue to be true to the game then I could be one of the greatest players to ever play this game. I just always believed that.

—postgame press conference, December 30, 2022

Part II

ON THE COURT

Cleveland

Cavaliers

A YEAR AGO I was watching this at the start of
the season. Now I'm finally here. It's a dream.
This will never get old. When it does, that's when
I'll stop playing.

—on playing his first NBA game, ESPN

I NEVER WANTED to leave Cleveland. My heart
will always be around that area. But I also felt
like this is the greatest challenge for me, is to
move on.

—*The Decision*, July 8, 2010

EDITORIAL NOTE: This quotation is from the first time James
left Cleveland, hoping to win a championship with the Miami
Heat, which he hadn't managed to do in seven years with the
Cavaliers.

I'M GOING TO have to teach, lead, and inspire these guys. But my number one goal is to win a championship here. I think it would be the greatest achievement of my life as far as on the court.

—Akron Beacon-Journal, August 9, 2014

> EDITORIAL NOTE: This quotation is from the month after James announced he would return to Cleveland for his second run with the Cavaliers.

JUST TWO YEARS ago I decided to go back home. And my main goal was to bring a championship to a place that hadn't seen one in over fifty-plus years. And to be able to bring it back to the hometown and do something that a lot of people didn't expect but we believed in, it meant everything.

—The Ellen Show, September 7, 2016

THIS WAS BIGGER for me than the first and the second because of everything it represents.

—on winning his Cleveland championship,
Sports Illustrated, **August 2016**

EDITORIAL NOTE: James won two championships over his four years with Miami before returning to Cleveland, where he finally won a championship in 2016.

I WANTED TO have a great time, I wanted to dance—I couldn't. I just had nothing left in me. I gave everything I had to that game. I gave everything I had to that series, to that game.

—*Road Trippin'* podcast, December 2017

LIFE. LIFE JUST changes. You have a mission and you have more goals that you want to set out, you know? When I won a championship here, I didn't think that I would go anywhere, because I felt like I was complete. And then I realized that I still wanted to, I wanted to reach another level. I wanted to reach another level, so it wasn't done. My life goal wasn't complete.

—on what changed to make him leave Cleveland again, *The Athletic*, February 19, 2022

Miami Heat

IN THIS FALL, this is very tough, in this fall I'm going to take my talents to South Beach and join the Miami Heat.

—*The Decision*, ESPN, July 8, 2010

I PLAY THE game fun, joyful. . . . That's what I lost last year. Going through my first seven years in the NBA I was always the "liked one" and to be on the other side—they call it the dark side or the villain or whatever they call it—it was definitely challenging for myself.

—on being viewed as the "villain" post–*The Decision*, ESPN, December 6, 2011

IT BASICALLY TURNED me into somebody I wasn't. You start to hear "the villain," now you have to be the villain, you know, and I started to buy into it. I started to play the game . . . angry.

—ESPN, December 6, 2011

EVERYBODY GONNA **critique** everything that you do no matter what you do. . . . My first year in Miami I wanted to prove everybody wrong, and I literally lost myself in the moment . . . and afterwards we lost because I wasn't even there.

—*The Shop UNINTERRUPTED* **podcast, March 2022**

CRITIQUE (verb): criticize

WE KNOW WE'RE not going to be able to bury teams every day. . . . Will we win by 20 points-plus every game? No, but that's our mentality.

—*South Florida Sun-Sentinel,* **November 5, 2010**

THE BEST THING that happened to me last year was us losing the finals. And me playing the way I played, it was the best thing to ever happen to me in my career, because . . . I got back to the basics. It **humbled** me. I knew what it was going to have to take, and I was going to have to change as a basketball player and I was going to have to change as a person to get what I wanted.

—*Ottowa Citizen*, July 23, 2012

HUMBLED (verb): reminded of one's own shortcomings

BEING A LEADER of my household, a leader of Miami, a leader of Team USA. It's the same exact thing. You can sense when a guy is frustrated—maybe doesn't feel involved enough in the offense. As leader you go over to him, you know, "How can I help?" Because at the end of the day, we all have one common goal—and that's to be great.

—*GQ*, February 18th, 2014

FROM THE TIME me and D-Wade got together, I just told him: "Just throw it anywhere, I'll go get it. Anywhere you throw it, I'll go get it." And that's what it was.

—on James and Wade playing together, ESPN

EDITORIAL NOTE: James and Dwyane Wade became friends when they entered the NBA draft together in 2003, and finally played together when James transferred to Miami, creating the powerhouse "Big Three" with fellow Miami player Chris Bosh. James and Wade maintained their famous friendship even after James left to go back to Cleveland.

THE CHAMPIONSHIP LASTS (he snaps his fingers) just like that. The confetti rains, you go into the locker room, pop the champagne, you do the media, you have the parade, and then it's over. It's over.

—*Honolulu Star-Advertiser*, October 29, 2013

Los Angeles Lakers

THIS IS A historic **franchise** and, to be a part of this, is something that I'll be able to talk about, and my grandkids and kids will be able to talk about that their "paw paw" or their "dad" played for the Los Angeles Lakers.

—**postgame press conference, October 11, 2020**

FRANCHISE (NOUN): a team and its entire organization, often tied to its historical significance

I THINK PERSONALLY thinking I have something to prove fuels me. . . . It fueled me over this last year-and-a-half since the injury. It fueled me because no matter what I've done in my career to this point, there's still rumblings of doubt.

—*Sports Illustrated*, **October 26, 2020**

IT'S MY RESPONSIBILITY to put this team in a position to be successful. . . . They look at me as a leader. And it's my job, not only on the floor to get guys opportunities, get them great looks, but to inspire them, as well. To show them that I'm not slowing down, even at this stage of my career.

—*New York Times,* March 9, 2020

WE PLAY GAMES without the fans? Nah, that's impossible. . . . I ain't playing if you don't have the fans in the crowd. That's who I play for.

—*New York Times,* March 9, 2020

EDITORIAL NOTE: When the COVID-19 pandemic halted the 2019–20 NBA season, the NBA opted to create a "bubble" to allow the final season games and playoffs to continue. The players were isolated at Disney World hotels and fans were not permitted at the games.

WE WERE ALL excited to get back, we were excited to play basketball again. I mean, we stopped playing in March. So we were all excited. But you don't really know what you are getting yourself into until you get inside the bubble and they tell you, "That right there, you cannot go outside that gate."

—*Road Trippin'* podcast, December 2020

IT MEANS SOMETHING. Something more than just a uniform. It represents an individual who gave the **franchise** twenty years of his blood, sweat, and tears and his dedication to his craft, both on and off the floor, to make that franchise be proud of him, and hopefully vice versa.

—on "Black Mamba" alternative uniforms post–Kobe Bryant's death, ESPN, October 7, 2020

EDITORIAL NOTE: Kobe Bryant spent all twenty years of his career with the LA Lakers and won five championships. He gave himself the nickname "Black Mamba," and after he died in a helicopter crash in January 2020, Lakers players wore Black Mamba jerseys in his honor.

YOU PLAY THE game the right way, and I think the basketball gods kind of give back to you. . . . We play hard. We fight. We scrap, and then live with the results and go from there. So we've given ourselves a good chance just to be the best team we can be.

—*The Athletic*, January 8, 2023

THIS WAS AN unbelievable achievement for our **franchise**, an unbelievable achievement for myself, what I was able to do for this team and what this team was able to do for me. And I want more. I'm not settled, and I'm not satisfied.

—on winning the 2020 NBA championship, *Road Trippin'* podcast, December 2020

WHEN I PLAYED for Miami, I rooted for the Marlins and I rooted for the Dolphins. Not saying they were my favorite teams, but at the end of the day I root for them and I want them to be as great as they can be. When I was in Cleveland, I rooted for the Browns. . . . We root for our **respective** clubs, because when we win, and we all win, it brings so much more joy to our communities, just a positive influence. Now that I'm here playing for the Lakers, besides the Clippers, I root for everybody.

—*Road Trippin'* podcast, December 2020

RESPECTIVE (adj.): particular, individual

EDITORIAL NOTE: The Marlins are Miami's Major League Baseball team, and the Dolphins are their NFL team. The Browns are the NFL team based in Cleveland. The Clippers are another NBA team in LA, and are rivals of the Lakers.

IT DOESN'T MATTER where it happens if you win a championship. . . . A bubble, Miami, Golden State—it doesn't matter. When you get to this point, it's one of the greatest feelings in the world for a basketball player to be able to win at the highest level.

—*New York Times*, October 11, 2020

Achievements

You guys don't know me by now? I don't play for individual stats. I play to win.

—*Miami Herald*, February 13, 2011

I gave everything that I had. I pour my heart, my blood, my sweat, my tears into this game. And, against all odds, I don't know why we want to take the hardest road, I don't know why the man above give me the hardest role, but the man above don't put you in situations that you can't handle.

—on coming back from a three-game deficit in the 2016 finals, postgame interview, December 24, 2016

It's something I never set out to do. I'm not even a score-first guy when it comes to playing basketball. I love getting my teammates involved and seeing my teammates be excited about scoring and me getting **assists**.

—on reaching 30,000 career points, NBA.com,
January 23, 2018

ASSISTS (noun): the action of a player helping their teammate score

EDITORIAL NOTE: Players can be described as "score-first" or "pass-first," depending on whether their strategy typically involves trying to score or trying to pass to another teammate.

WHEN IT COMES to the record, I felt pretty good, I felt in a good rhythm and once I get in a good rhythm I feel like I make any shot on the floor. . . . I was able to get it and it touched nothing but the bottom of the net and that was pretty cool.

—on becoming the leading scorer in NBA history, ESPN, February 8, 2023

I WANTED TO be the Rookie of the Year my rookie year, I wanted to be an All-Star, I wanted to win championships, I wanted to be the MVP of the league, I wanted to be Defensive Player of the Year. . . . I never, ever was like, "I wanna break the all-time scoring record." It's never ever been a thought of mine and the fact that I'm like literally right here, it's mind-blowing.

—ABC News, February 8, 2023

NOT AT ALL. I didn't get to this point in my career by thinking about records or how many points I have.... Maybe when I get super-duper close, maybe it will be at the back of my mind or the front of my mind. But I never put that type of pressure on myself. I just go and play.

—when asked if he thought about breaking Kareem Abdul-Jabbar's career scoring record, *New York Times*, February 1, 2023

> EDITORIAL NOTE: Kareem Abdul-Jabbar—nineteen-time NBA All-Star and six-time NBA champion—held the league scoring record from 1984 until James beat it in 2023.

I SEE IT and I smirk. When they talk about the best scorers who ever played the game, my name never comes up. They have no choice now.

—on breaking the NBA all-time scoring record, ESPN, February 7, 2023

LAST WEEK MESSED around and got a triple..... I mean a Scoring Record! Man what!!! This is still not hitting me yet. So surreal!! Wow wow wow man!! To all my fans who captured that moment there inside Crypto Arena that night (YOU'RE AMAZING & THANK YOU) and to all my fans all over the United States and The World (YOU'RE AMAZING & THANK YOU).

—**Instagram, February 14, 2023**

EDITORIAL NOTE: A triple, or triple-double, is when a player scores ten or more in three categories: points, assists, steals, rebounds, etc. In the first sentence of the quote, James is referencing a lyric from an Ice Cube song, "It Was a Good Day," but inserting his own achievement, when he surpassed the all-time scoring record.

The Game

I IMPROVED OVER the course of my career. So, there's never been a ceiling too high or I've never put a ceiling on what I can accomplish.

—ESPN, November 3, 2017

EVERY DAY IS a dream. I'm so blessed that this game of basketball has taken this kid from Akron around the globe. I never take a single moment for granted.

—Instagram, September 14, 2016

LEADERSHIP IS NOT a one-day thing. . . . Leadership is consistent. And I believe having **longevity** in the space I'm in is also consistency as well, not only on the floor but off the floor as well.

—*The Tim Ferriss Show*, November 27, 2018

LONGEVITY (noun): the ability to exist or last for a long time

IT COMES BACK to that patience, of learning [the players'] mindsets, learning how can you get the most out of them, what triggers them to be their best, what triggers them to not be their best. You learn that over time.

—*The Tim Ferriss Show*, November 27, 2018

IF YOU CHALLENGE me to score, I'm going to score. And at the same time I'm going to keep my guys involved. I play for the team.

—*Road Trippin'* podcast, December 2020

THE ONLY THING that bothers me is when I'm not able to play because of an injury. That bothers me when I'm not able to be on the floor. Because I never know if it was that game or that city that a kid was coming to come see me and I'm not playing in that game. That's the only thing that kinda bothers me.

—*The Shop UNINTERRUPTED* podcast, March 2022

I GIVE EVERYTHING to the game and I hope it continues to give back to me!

—Twitter, January 17, 2013

I'VE ALWAYS LOVE[D] seeing the success of my teammates!! Seeing my teammates score always meant more to me than me scoring! I can't do anything without those guys every single night. Their hardwork, dedication, professionalism, etc, etc has put me in the position I am today.

—Instagram, February 24, 2015

WHO KNEW A three-year-old boy's dream and a Little Tikes hoop could lead to all this?

—Instagram, April 3, 2016

MY LOVE FOR this game is insane and drive[s] me crazy! Which I LOVE!! Nothing to me is better than the process of feeling uncomfortable as u try and push to improve on your skill/talent. I have no ceiling and I refuse to fall into the trap of **complacency**!

—Instagram, August 23, 2017

COMPLACENCY (noun): the state of being overly comfortable or satisfied with one's own performance

TO FEEL THAT **adversity**, to feel that tension is what brings out the best in us, you know. Your whole motivation besides trying to win the game, obviously, is shutting up the opposing fans and opposing crowd and making them go home and get no sleep because of you.

—*Jimmy Kimmel Live,* July 14, 2021

ADVERSITY (noun): a state of hardship or difficulty

I JUST FEEL so good about the game. I feel like I owe it to the game, as long as I could go out and still play at a high level, I feel like it's important for me to continue to inspire the youth, continue to inspire my teammates, try to inspire myself. And I still have championship **aspiration**.

—ESPN, February 7, 2023

ASPIRATION (noun): desire for success and achievement

SOMETIMES I WAKE up and I'm like, "Oh, I ain't gonna make it tonight, I just feel it. These twenty years have got to me tonight. It ain't gonna be good tonight." And then I get out on the floor and I'm running past, you know, twenty-one-year-olds, jumping higher than twenty-three-year-olds, and I feel real good on how I'm playing the game, not only physically but more importantly just, like, mentally.

—ESPN, February 7, 2023

CHEMISTRY IS ALWAYS very key.... In my experience I've been able to be a part of both where you have some inexperienced lineups or inexperienced teams.... And then, obviously, I've been a part of teams that have been through so many battles that **adversity** meant nothing, you know, because that's when you literally, like, thrive [is] in those moments, those adverse moments.

—**postgame press conference, December 17, 2022**

I'M A TEAM-FIRST guy when it comes to understanding that you can't be great in this league without great teammates, great coaches, that prepare [you] every single day to be great.

—ESPN, February 8, 2023

I KNOW WE win. But I don't really know what happened.

—on watching tape, *Sports Illustrated*, August 2, 2016

TO BE ABLE to play at this level, you know, twenty years in, and the minutes I've played, the games I've played . . . to still be at the **apex** of my game, it's a pretty surreal feeling. So, you know, hopefully I can continue it, but at the end of the day it's just been a pleasure to be in this league for twenty years. . . . I've had a hell of a ride.

—*House of Highlights,* February 8, 2023

APEX (noun): the highest point

Part III

OFF THE COURT

Philanthropy

I KNOW A lot comes with being a professional athlete. That's also being a role model to a lot of kids that look up to me. This automatically comes with it. And I have nothing but time for kids. I could easily be at home and just relaxing. . . . But the opportunity to be here and giving back to these kids, I'm happy to do it.

—on donating to the Boys & Girls Clubs of America and spending time with the children who benefited through the donation, ESPN, March 2, 2011

TO BE AN African American kid and grow up in the inner city with a single-parent mother and not being financially stable and to make it to where I've made it today, I think I've defeated the odds, and I want every kid to know that and everybody to know that the youth, they can do it as well.

—ESPN, February 18, 2018

TOMORROW IS GOING to be one of the greatest moments (if not the greatest) of my life when we open the #IPROMISE School. This skinny kid from Akron who missed 83 days of school in the 4th grade had big dreams...big dreams for the kids in Akron to give them everything they could need to find their passion, give back to our community, and change the world!! This school is that. The people are that. Akron is that.

—Twitter, July 29, 2018

EDITORIAL NOTE: After researching high school dropout rates in Akron in 2011, James created the I PROMISE initiative, which eventually developed into the I PROMISE School, which is an Akron public school aimed at at-risk children in grades one through eight and is supported by the LeBron James Family Foundation.

IT MEANS EVERYTHING to not only myself, not only to my foundation, but to my hometown. And those 240 kids that's in there right now, I walked the same streets as those kids, I had the same dreams, the same nightmares, the same upbringing as those kids, so I know everything that they're going through. And for me to be able to have a thought about having an at-risk school and then have it come to **fruition** and us opening a month ago. . . . By 2021, we'll have grades first through eighth, over 1,200 kids. It's a dream come true for me and I hope that the dream coming true for me will make their dreams become a reality. It's unbelievable.

—*The Ellen Show,* September 12, 2018

FRUITION (noun): coming to be, being realized

So WE'VE GIVEN the opportunity for parents in these households that didn't graduate high school to get an opportunity to graduate, get a GED as well so they can feel like, parents do their work, kids do their work, they feel like, listen, we all empowered.

—*The Daily Show,* August 17, 2016

EDITORIAL NOTE: GED stands for general educational development. Adults who didn't finish high school can study and take the GED exam to earn their diploma.

YOU KNOW, FOR me, personally, I know where
I come from, growing up in inner city in Akron,
Ohio. And I know the challenges that kids
have. And for our society to become as great as
it should be, I think it starts from the ground
up. And it starts in our communities, our own
communities, going back into our communities,
using our resources, using our knowledge.
Anybody can lend money or anybody can go give
an appearance, but I think actually being there
and them seeing you gives them—it gives the kids
hope. And without the kids we have no future.

—*The Daily Show,* August 17, 2016

THESE KIDS ARE doing an unbelievable job,
better than we all expected. . . . When we first
started, people knew I was opening a school for
kids. Now people are going to really understand
the lack of education they had before they
came to our school. People are going to finally
understand what goes on behind our doors.

—*New York Times,* April 12, 2019

I HAD THE vision of wanting to give back to my community. The people around every day are helping that vision come to life. . . . Half the battle is trying to engage them and show that there's always going to be somebody looking out for them.

—*New York Times,* **April 12, 2019**

WHEN WE STARTED this work in education with my foundation, we never dreamed we'd be owning buildings and developing new properties. . . . As we dug deeper into the work, we learned what it takes to create real, visible change. And that's listening to what our community needs and then rolling up our sleeves and getting to work.

—*New York Times,* **March 10, 2021**

IT MEANS SO much because, as a kid growing up in the inner city and a lot of African American kids, you don't really think past high school. ... You hear high school all the time, and you graduate high school, and then you never think past that because either it's not possible or your family's not financially stable to even be able to support a kid going to college.

—on his 4-year college scholarship for I PROMISE kids,
ESPN, August 14, 2015

HUMBLED & PROUD to announce the establishment of the LeBron James Family Foundation I PROMISE Institute at The University of Akron. Scholarships weren't enough. We're investing our time, talent, and resources every day with our team, partners, and UA to give my kids every opportunity possible for them to be successful. I won't be satisfied with them just getting to college or tech school. We need them to graduate. This is our home. This is my home.

—Instagram, October 12, 2016

> **HUMBLED** (adj.): not boastful or full of oneself

> **EDITORIAL NOTE:** James offered scholarships to his I PROM-
> ISE students to attend the University of Akron after finishing
> high school. The I PROMISE Institute at the university is meant
> to provide resources and help support those students through
> college to give them a better chance at graduating.

I BELIEVE IN order for us to **ultimately** be as
great as we can be as a nation that all of us have
to go back into our communities and lend our
hand. It starts brick by brick. It starts person by
person. Family by family. Kid by kid.

—on the LeBron James Family Foundation, ESPN,
August 17, 2016

> **ULTIMATELY** (adv.): in the end, eventually

Advocacy
and
Activism

I KNOW MY purpose and it's for damn sure bigger than just dribbling a basketball.

—**Instagram, February 17, 2018**

GROWING UP IN the inner city, seeing how **underprivileged** Black people are, I always felt like if I had an opportunity to be able to have any type of platform I always wanted to give back to that, I always wanted to be able to use my voice, and the people that grow up like me to be able to understand that we do have power, we do have an opportunity to make people understand that there is good in love.

—**postgame press conference, January 17, 2023**

BASKETBALL IS OUR vehicle but equality is our mission – stand for something positive and do what you can to make a difference!!

—**Instagram, February 26, 2018**

WHEN GEORGE FLOYD was murdered and all of us organized in the streets and on social media to demand action, More Than a Vote came together. We are a **coalition** of Black athletes using our influence to educate, energize and protect Black voters.

—Instagram, August 17, 2020

COALITION (noun): a group of people working toward a common goal

EDITORIAL NOTE: George Floyd was a Black man killed by a white police officer in May 2020 when the officer knelt on his neck for over nine minutes. The murder led to widespread protests against police brutality and racism.

WE ALL HAVE moments in our lives where we know who we are and we know what we're about. And it's about growth. I've grown over the course of my career. I've grown over the course of being an 18-year-old kid that came into the league in 2003, to a 35-year-old man that's a husband and a father of three kids. I've grown to know who I am and what I stand for. And it's not just about me, it's about my people. That's why I'm leading the charge.

—on his More Than a Vote initiative, *New York Times,*
October 21, 2020

EVERYONE IN CALIFORNIA: call your politicians and tell them to support SB 206! This law is a GAME CHANGER. College athletes can responsibly get paid for what they do and the billions they create.

—Twitter, September 5, 2019

> **EDITORIAL NOTE:** Student athletes have traditionally not been allowed to profit from their name, image, or likeness. For example, a student athlete could not make money from the sale of jerseys with their name on the back. California Senate Bill 206 was introduced to change that, and it went into effect in 2021.

ONE OF MY first goals is to continue to inspire the youth to want to play this game of basketball or be better in whatever that they do.... Inspire millions no matter what they've gone through in their lives at that point in time, they can always overcome it.

—postgame press conference, June 21, 2013

WITHOUT THOSE GUYS [athletes such as Bill Russell, Kareem Abdul-Jabbar, and Oscar Robertson] standing for something that was more than dribbling a basketball . . . I'm not sitting here talking to you.

—*Shut Up and Dribble,* **November 3, 2018**

EDITORIAL NOTE: Russell, Abdul-Jabbar, and Robertson were all championship-winning Black basketball players in the '60s, '70s, and '80s who were also involved in activism off the court.

IT MEANS SOMETHING . . . something more than just a uniform.

—**on wearing warm-up shirts that read "VOTE,"**
New York Times, **October 11, 2020**

YES, WE WANT you to go out and vote, but we're also going to give you the tutorial. . . . We're going to give you the background of how to vote and what they're trying to do, the other side, to stop you from voting.

—New York Times, July 30, 2020

WHEN YOU WAKE up and you're Black, that is what it is. . . . It shouldn't be a movement. It should be a lifestyle. This is who we are. And we understand that. And we know that for one step that someone else might have to take, or for one yard someone else may have to take, we know we've got to take five more steps. . . . I don't like the word "movement" because, unfortunately, in America and in society, there ain't been no damn movement for us.

—New York Times, July 24, 2020

IT WAS A message to the family. That I'm sorry for their loss, sorry to his wife. That's what it's about. I think everybody else gets caught up in everything else besides who's really feeling it, and that's the family. That's what it's about.

—on wearing an "I Can't Breathe" shirt after the killing of Eric Garner, ESPN, December 8, 2014

EDITORIAL NOTE: Eric Garner was a Black man killed by a white police officer in 2014 when the officer pinned him on the ground in an illegal chokehold. Garner repeated the words "I can't breathe" multiple times until he lost consciousness.

THAT'S HOW AMERICA has been for a long time and [it] ain't going to change, but what will change is how guys in power [respond]. And what will change for me, and what has already changed, is I will continue to speak up for my people no matter if [society] likes it or not.

—ESPN, February 25, 2022

YOU'RE NOT A criminal because you put a hood over the top of your head. It's a uniform for us. That's what we do. That's what we wear. We don't have the luxury of wearing suits or having button-downs. We don't have the means to get sweaters and things of that nature. Our uniform is T-shirts, hoodies, and shorts. That's our uniform growing up as Black kids in the inner city.

—on the killing of Trayvon Martin, ESPN,
February 25, 2022

EDITORIAL NOTE: Trayvon Martin was a Black teenager who was fatally shot by a neighbor who viewed him as suspicious as he walked back to his father's house from a convenience store. The case cast light on racial profiling, particularly aimed at Black men and teens who wear hooded sweatshirts, as Martin had that night.

PART THREE *Advocacy and Activism*

LEBRON IN HIS OWN WORDS   **77**

Hate, in America, especially for an African American, is living every day. Even though it's concealed most of the time—people will hide their faces and will say things about you and then when they see you they smile in your face— it's alive every single day. And I think back to Emmett Till's mom, actually. It's kind of one of the first things I thought of. And the reason that she had an open casket is because she wanted to show the world what her son went through as far as the hate crime, and being Black in America.

No matter how much money you have, no matter how famous you are, no matter how many people admire you, being Black in America is tough. And we've got a long way to go for us as a society, and for us as African Americans, until we feel equal in America.

—**pre-game press conference, June 1, 2017**

EDITORIAL NOTE: Emmett Till was a fourteen-year-old Black boy who was visiting relatives in Mississippi in 1955 when white men kidnapped and brutally murdered him. Till's mother famously opted for an open casket so the world could see what had been done to her son. The story and images sparked national attention on the civil rights movement.

When you're born African American, you always got to do things more than the norm just because you're Black.... We understand that we have to work even extra hard because there's just always a "prove" thing. We always got to try to prove ourselves.

—ESPN, November 19, 2017

AS THE PLAYERS, to be able to use the NBA platform and us be able to go out there and speak about **systemic** racism, police brutality, voter suppression, everything that was going on, gave us an opportunity.... Strength in numbers. We actually saw that in the bubble.

—*Road Trippin'* podcast, December 2020

SYSTEMIC (adj.): dependent on social, economic, or political parts of a society such that they cannot be separated from it

EDITORIAL NOTE: Voter suppression is a series of strategies that political groups use to try to keep certain groups of people from voting in order to affect the results of an election. It has historically made it more difficult for racial minorities to vote.

YOU WANT TO see all this change, but I felt like those conversations and that change needed to happen before we stepped back on the floor. And we had a conversation where two or three guys from each **respective** team, the coaches, and we had a huge Zoom call with the owners, all thirty owners. To talk about some of the changes, or some of the things that we can do to help create change while we're still playing the game. Because a lot of people was saying, "Well, once you guys get to playing basketball, you guys are going to forget about us." And I didn't want that to happen. . . . I wanted to see real change.

—*Road Trippin'* podcast, December 2020

ANY ONE OF us in this world, or in America, where we live in, if you do something that harms other people, you are held **accountable**. And we felt like at that point in time, the police were not being held accountable.

—Road Trippin' podcast, December 2020

ACCOUNTABLE (adj.): responsible for

ONE OF MY biggest goals was like, how ... can I create voice and power for us: as Black creators, as Black people?

—The Shop UNINTERRUPTED podcast, October 2022

MY WHOLE MISSION in life is to speak for my people.

—The Shop UNINTERRUPTED podcast, June 2022

To my brothers and sisters in sports and arts. We have incredible influence in our community. We need to use this moment to demand change. I gotta be honest...I struggle with what to demand because so damn much needs to change.

—**Instagram, June 23, 2020**

Black voters came through...again. Be proud as hell but do not stop! We must stay organized and keep working. We just tipping off.

—**Instagram, November 6, 2020**

THERE IS NO place for **misogyny**, sexism, and racism in any work place. Don't matter if you own the team or play for the team. We hold our league up as an example of our values and this aint it.

—on misogyny and racism from then-owner of the Phoenix Suns Robert Sarver, Facebook, September 14, 2022

MISOGYNY (noun): prejudice against women

AT THE END of the day, it's very rare that you can play professional sports but be known for something bigger than that when you're done. It's very rare.

—*Road Trippin'* podcast, December 2017

Family

BASKETBALL HAS GIVEN me a lot, has taken me all over the world, has inspired a lot of people, but you know for me being a father is even more **dynamic**, way more driven than the game.

—ESPN, February 8, 2023

DYNAMIC (adj.): often changing or progressing

IN ORDER FOR me to be able to accomplish what I've done over these two decades, I had to have the rock and the support that I got from Savannah. There's no way that I would've been able to enjoy these moments or to be able to commit to my craft—she's allowed me to do this.

—NBA on TNT, February 19, 2023

EDITORIAL NOTE: Savannah and LeBron began dating in high school and married in 2013. She has kept a relatively low profile throughout their marriage but has championed multiple mentorship and charity projects in their hometown of Akron.

I TRY TO set an example of how I treat their mother on a day-to-day basis, how I treat their grandmothers, you know, how I treat their little sister. How I treat others with kind[ness] and patience, so hopefully I can **instill** life skills in them, so when they walk out in the real world they'll be able to behave themselves like men.

—**ESPN, February 8, 2023**

INSTILL (verb): teach, little by little

I WANTED TO be a part of the statistics that breaks the mode of fathers running out on their kids. That was something that I obviously went through and I knew from Day 1 that wasn't going to be me.

—*Cleveland.com*, **June 19, 2016**

HERE'S TO ALL the fathers that didn't have the blueprint but figured it out along the way!!
🖤🙏👑

—**Twitter, December 12, 2022**

YOU CAN'T HAVE any expectations just because you're ... LeBron's son. You have to be even more cautious, because you just don't know. And that is a scary thing, being a Black father with a kid that drives. ... These kids are so well known, and they're leaving the house, and [our] daughter's in school.

—*Sports Illustrated*, **August 30, 2022**

WE DON'T EVEN really talk about the future too much. I put it in the air because I like to talk to the basketball gods out there and see if things can come to **fruition**. I've always set out goals in my career, talked to the basketball gods, and they've listened to all of them. Hopefully they can listen to this last one, too.

—**on playing in the NBA with his oldest son, Bronny,**
Sports Illustrated, **August 30, 2022**

I'VE ALWAYS LOOKED at parenthood, business, and basketball as kind of being the same thing when you are a leader. You have all these different personalities; you have to figure out how to put these personalities in the right place to maximize the team.... As a parent, yes, I have three kids and you give them the same structure, but you can't coach them all the same because they are all different people.

—*Kneading Dough: The Podcast*, **March 5, 2019**

I JUST TOLD my wife the other day that I apologize to her. . . . Because the journey that I'm on to want to be the greatest to ever play this game to the point where no one ever forgets what I accomplished, I've at times lost the fact of how important you are to this whole thing. . . . I said I want you to understand that along this journey while I'm playing this game that there will be times where I lose the fact of how important you and my three kids are—my babies are—because of how **indebted** I am in trying to be cemented in something that will last forever.

—*Road Trippin'* podcast, March 2017

indebted (adj.): owing gratitude to

THE ONLY REASON why I can do what I do at the highest level both on and off the floor is because my best friend got my back regardless the outcome! I'm just the car, she's the engine! Appreciate you Wonder Woman aka Queen

—Instagram, November 14, 2019

BLACK BOYS NEED Black men in their lives.
Doesn't even need to be their father. Thank you
to every strong, admirable Black man who I had
as a kid.

—**Twitter, March 29, 2018**

BRONNY, BRYCE, AND Zhuri, my three kids.
They're my treasures, my gems. . . . Bronny,
Bryce, and Z [make] me happy, make me smile
every single day.

—*I Promise Podcast*, **October 4, 2022**

[THE KIDS] WOULD never understand that
there's a bottom. That's the challenge of a parent
every single day that I have to juggle with: how do
I raise my kids knowing that they'll never feel or
understand what their father went through? But
you give them challenges, and at the end of the
day they are going to walk their own path.

—*Kneading Dough: The Podcast*, **March 5, 2019**

[MY MOTHER] WAS always a rock. No matter what was going on, she was always a rock and very patient with the process, and I've taken that not only to being a father but in life in general; I always preach this process thing.

—*The Tim Ferriss Show*, November 27, 2018

MY FAMILY IS everything to me. And it's a personal **mantra** of mine to always be loyal to my family. . . . A family is not a bed of roses, it comes with thorns, and you have to understand that.

—*The Tim Ferriss Show*, November 27, 2018

MANTRA (noun): a strong personal belief

MY LAST YEAR will be played with my son. Wherever Bronny is at, that's where I'll be. I would do whatever it takes to play with my son for one year. It's not about the money at that point.

—*The Athletic,* **February 19, 2022**

Part IV

LEGACY

Image

IT'S ALWAYS PRETTY cool to see, the guys that come into our league and they said their favorite player growing up was LeBron James. That means something to me because I feel like I have so much more to do than just playing the game of basketball.

—postgame press conference, February 20, 2022

THEN, WHEN MY grandkids show up at some point I'll be able to show them some footage of what their granddad was able to accomplish when he played the game of basketball.

—postgame press conference, February 20, 2022

I THINK **legacy** will speak for itself. Who I am as a man and what I do off the floor defines my legacy more than what I do on the court and that's just how I've always thought about it, but I don't really get caught up into it too much.

—*Today Show*, July 6, 2015

LEGACY (noun): what someone leaves behind, what people remember of them

I'M THE BIGGEST voice that my hometown has ever seen. . . . I'm the biggest figure that my hometown has ever seen. I do know that. I can see that. The responsibility of being the inspiration and the light for my community—it's much greater than hitting a jump shot.

—*GQ*, February 18, 2014

EDITORIAL NOTE: A jump shot in basketball is when a player jumps straight up into the air with the ball raised above their head and then launches the ball toward the net in an attempt to score.

I DON'T [CARE] what nobody says. Our quest and our journey is not **predicated** on what everybody said. You going to have five people that love you out of 10. Then you have five people that hate you out of 10. That's just the way of the land. No matter what you do.

—*Sports Illustrated*, August 30, 2022

PREDICATED (verb): founded or based on

I WOULD HOPE that people take away that because I was able to play the game at such a high level, that none of that mattered to me because my **legacy** off the floor was more impactful.

—*I Promise Podcast*, October 4, 2022

I JUST FEEL so good about the game. I feel like I owe it to the game, as long as I could go out and play at a high level, I feel like it's important for me to continue to inspire the youth, continue to inspire my teammates, try to inspire myself, and I still have championship **aspiration**.

—ESPN, February 7, 2023

I KNEW WHEN I got drafted as an eighteen-year-old kid that I could play the game of basketball and play it at a high level even against grown men. One thing I didn't know is the success I would have. I prayed on the success, I worked my tail off for the success, but had no idea the success [I would have], and it's just been a very **humbling** and **gratifying**, you know, journey, and I hope people have enjoyed it with me.

—ESPN, February 7, 2023

GRATIFYING (adj.): pleasing, rewarding

LOVE ME OR hate me but at the end of the day you
will RESPECT me!

—**Twitter, April 14, 2016**

HOPEFULLY I MADE an impact enough so people
appreciate what I did, and still appreciate what
I did off the floor as well, even when I'm done....
But I don't live for that. I live for my family, for my
friends and my community that needs that voice.

—***New York Times***, **February 4, 2023**

Philosophy

I DON'T NEED motivation from anybody in this league. I motivate myself.

—*New York Times*, June 4, 2021

I LIKE TO throw things out in the airwaves, but I'm not one to [say] what's going to happen in the next two to three years. I am a **visionary**, but I'm also a guy that lives in the moment.

—*Sports Illustrated*, August 30, 2022

> VISIONARY (noun): someone who has ideas for the future

I FEEL LIKE I could play for quite a while. So it's all up to my body, but more importantly, my mind. If my mind can stay sharp and fresh and motivated, then the sky's not even a limit for me. I can go beyond that. But we shall see.

—*Sports Illustrated*, August 30, 2022

I DON'T WANT to say it ever becomes too much, but there are times when I wish I could do normal things. . . . I wish I could just walk outside. . . . I wish I could just, like, walk into a movie theater and sit down and go to the concession stand and get popcorn. I wish I could just go to an amusement park just like regular people. I wish I could go to Target sometimes and walk into Starbucks and have my name on the cup just like regular people. . . . I'm not sitting here complaining about it, of course not. But it can be challenging at times.

—*New York Times*, February 4, 2023

EVERYONE LIKES TO have their me time. And, of course, I'm one of those guys. But for the most part, with my energy, I don't like being alone. I like being around people and having fun and laughing and being able to give my energy to other people also.

—*Miami Herald*, February 20, 2011

IT'S NOT ABOUT making the shot. . . . It's about having a belief of just taking it, for one, and living with the result.

—*New York Times*, September 27, 2020

I'M VERY MOTIVATED. But I'm right now not in the talking-about-it mode. I've been very quiet this summer for a reason. My mother always told me, "Don't talk about it, be about it." So that's where I'm at.

—ESPN, September 17, 2020

EDITORIAL NOTE: Earlier in 2019, James had suffered an injury that forced him to miss seventeen games, and the Lakers did not make the playoffs—James's first time missing them since 2005. But over the summer James healed and the team improved their lineup, and they went on to win the championship in 2020.

I PUT A lot of pressure on myself not to let my teammates down. At the end of the day, that's what it's all about for me. Maybe to a fault at times, I put so much pressure on myself.

—ESPN, June 15, 2011

[READING] JUST SLOWS my mind down. It just gives me another outlet. Throughout the playoffs all you think about is basketball. All you want to do is play basketball. But at the same time it can become a lot.

—*NBC Sports*, June 21, 2012

NO MATTER IF you come from the top of the top or you come from the bottom of the bottom, you still have a road to travel.

—*Kneading Dough: The Podcast*, March 5, 2019

I KNEW THAT money would allow me to access those things, but I never let money get in the way of the drive that I had to get to the top.

—*Kneading Dough: The Podcast*, **March 5, 2019**

NO MATTER HOW many times I fail, I'll always be ready for the next opportunity.

—**Twitter, March 1, 2011**

WE DON'T NEED more LeBron's, we need more physical therapists, scientists, police officers, teachers, doctors, professors, physicists, computer engineers, etc!! I want every kid to know there is absolutely NO LIMIT to what you can be. Your dreams are there for you to EARN. The teacher/accountant/scientist/dr/etc is just as talented as any athlete, if not more. I can't even begin to tell you guys how many incredible men & women I work with who have never seen the court but are just as vital to our success as I am. There's no way my game is what it is without them. Open your heart & mind to the world around you. See the possible. Dream big. Then work your tail off and chase it.

—Instagram, April 1, 2017

I ALWAYS PREACH that the best teacher in life is experience, and it's okay for you to experience defeat. But when you are at a position where you might have to cross that **threshold** again, do you approach it the same way or do you learn from that?

—*The Tim Ferriss Show*, November 27, 2018

THRESHOLD (noun): a boundary or point at which something will happen

I TAKE THAT responsibility and I don't just talk about it, I actually do it as well. So when you come through on your word, it allows the guys that you are leading, male or female, to be able to say, "Okay, we can follow this person because he won't let us down." No matter if it's going good or bad. Every day is not a bed of roses and we understand that, and you have to be able to handle **adversity** as well.

—*Success! How I Did It*, May 11, 2017

FAITH IN YOUR own powers and confidence in your individual methods are essential to success.

—**Twitter, December 29, 2010**

IF LIFE WASN'T a struggle, there would be nothing to accomplish or overcome. The struggles in your life are positive.

—**Twitter, October 25, 2010**

STRUCTURE AND CONSISTENCY creates perfection. You shortcut, you come up short!

—**Twitter, March 6, 2016**

LET'S GO! UP and at it to workouts. 5:38am. No excuses! #SavageMode #StriveForGreatness

—**Twitter, August 18, 2017**

I THINK MY career has been like that. It's been like one of the great rides at Cedar Point in the sense that you know your stomach drop[s] at times, you're excited, you're yelling, sometimes you can't breathe, but you always wanna do it again.

—**ESPN, February 8, 2023**

> **EDITORIAL NOTE:** Cedar Point is an amusement park in Sandusky, Ohio, known for its many roller coasters.

MY LIFE'S MORE than just basketball… because there's a whole lot more to life! 🙏 …[I'm] hoping others go out & find their passion & purpose like I've found mine. Because to live a meaningful life requires more!! 🙌 💧

—**Facebook, February 16, 2023**

WHEN YOU PUT in the work, the results will happen. . . . If you didn't put in the work, that's when you get worried.

—*New York Times*, **August 21, 2020**

The GOAT

Debate

My MOTIVATION IS this ghost I'm chasing. The ghost played in Chicago.

—*Sports Illustrated*, August 2, 2016

EDITORIAL NOTE: The "ghost" James is referring to is Michael Jordan, who played for the Chicago Bulls in the '80s and '90s, winning six championships there, and became a global cultural icon. James is often compared to Jordan in the debate over who is the greatest basketball player ever, often called the "GOAT" (greatest of all time).

My CAREER IS totally different than Michael Jordan's. What I've gone through is totally different than what he went through. What he did was unbelievable, and I watched it unfold. I looked up to him so much. I think it's cool to put myself in position to be one of those great players, but if I can ever put myself in position to be the greatest player, that would be something extraordinary.

—*Sports Illustrated*, August 2, 2016

I'M NOT MJ, I'm LJ.

—Twitter, February 13, 2013

I WANT TO be, if not the greatest, one of the greatest to ever play this game, and I will continue to work for that and continue to put on this uniform and be the best I can be every night.

—postgame press conference, June 21, 2013

GOT LIKE 50 pictures of MJ on my wall—that's all you need to know about me. Got Iverson, McGrady, Magic, and Kobe on there, too. And myself. I'm on my wall.

—ESPN, December 23, 2002

EDITORIAL NOTE: Allen Iverson, Tracy McGrady, Magic Johnson, and Kobe Bryant were all highly successful NBA players with numerous All-Star appearances, championships, and scoring records.

IT'S NO COMPARISON to him. I think people always try to figure out ways or want to compare someone to someone. But you know, Mike is Mike and I'm LeBron and I'm trying to make my own name, make my own statement.

—*South Florida Sun-Sentinel,* February 15, 2013

You can debate who's the greatest of all time individually, things of that nature, and what they've done. But as far as the teams that's won two of the hardest championship in Lakers history, I've been a part of that.

—*Road Trippin'* podcast, December 2020

Being in the conversation so much about being a part of the all-time greats, it's always **humbling** to me. I really don't get caught up in the comparison.

—*Road Trippin'* podcast, June 2017

I always feel like I'm the best to ever play this game, but you know there's so many other great ones and I'm happy to just be a part of their journey.

—*House of Highlights,* February 8, 2023

Milestones

1984

- LeBron Raymone James (Sr.) is born on December 30, 1984, in Akron, Ohio, to Gloria Marie James and Anthony McClelland. His father is absent from his life, so he is raised by his sixteen-year-old single mother. They often move from one neighborhood to another as his mother seeks work.

1988

- James receives a kids' basketball hoop and ball on Christmas Day, thus introducing him to the game that will immortalize him in NBA history.

1993

- After being spotted playing football with some other kids, eight-year-old James is invited to play youth football by coach Bruce Kelker. James's mother says she can't pay for James's equipment or transport him to practice, but Kelker tells her he'll take care of everything, determined to get James on his new team. Kelker fosters James's talent, outfits him with everything he needs to play, and takes him to and from practice. However, when going to pick up James, he often discovers that James and his mother have once again moved. In response, Kelker invites James and his mother to live with him so his star player can attend games.

- Frank Walker, another local youth football coach, sees that space is growing tight in Kelker's household and, wanting to keep James in Akron with his mother and playing football, invites James to come live with his family, giving James his first taste of a stable home life. Here, James is formally introduced to the game of basketball by Walker and allowed to practice once he finishes all of his homework.

1997

- James wins his first MVP title for helping lead his team, the Shooting Stars, to victory in the twelve-and-younger division of the Youth Basketball of America national tournament.

1999

- James chooses to attend St. Vincent–St. Mary High School, a private Catholic school with a predominantly white student body, with his "Fab Four" friends he met while playing in the Amateur Athletic Union.

- As a freshman, James plays for the Fighting Irish on St. Vincent–St. Mary's varsity basketball team.

2000

- James helps lead the St. Vincent–St. Mary varsity basketball team to their first of three state titles and an undefeated 27–0 season.

2001

- James becomes the first high school sophomore to be named Ohio's Mr. Basketball.

- James leads the Fighting Irish varsity basketball team to their second consecutive state championship.

- He becomes the first high school sophomore to be selected for the *USA Today* All-USA First Team.

- James is featured in a *Slam* magazine article and praised as someone who "might just be the best high school basketball player in America right now."

2002

- At just seventeen years old, James appears on the cover of *Sports Illustrated* with the headline "The Chosen One."

- James is consecutively named Ohio's Mr. Basketball and selected for the *USA Today* All-USA First Team. He is also named the *USA Today* Player of the Year for boys' high school basketball.

- During his senior year, James makes his debut on national television playing against the top-ranked school in the country, Oak Hill Academy. The game is broadcast on ESPN2, and James's team wins 65–45, with James scoring 31 points.

2003

- James becomes the first person to win the title of Ohio's Mr. Basketball three years in a row.

- James finishes his high school basketball career with the Fighting Irish's third state title in the four years he plays on the team.

- James is selected for the *USA Today* All-USA First Team for the third year in a row, and is named the *USA Today* High School Player of the Year for the second year in a row.

- James is chosen as the first overall pick in the 2003 NBA draft for his hometown team, the Cleveland Cavaliers.

- He plays his first professional basketball game as a Cavalier on October 29 against the Sacramento Kings. The team loses 106–92, despite an impressive debut performance from James.

2004

- James becomes the first Cavalier and the youngest player ever to be named the NBA Rookie of the Year.

- James founds the LeBron James Family Foundation in his hometown of Akron, Ohio.

- James debuts on the U.S. Men's National Basketball Team at the Summer Olympics in Athens, Greece. However, Team USA finishes with a bronze medal—breaking a streak of winning gold in the Olympics since 1992.

- James's first child, LeBron Raymone "Bronny" James Jr., is born on October 6.

2005

- James plays in his first NBA All-Star Game, becoming the second-youngest player to participate in an All-Star Game.

2006

- James is once again selected to play in the NBA All-Star Game and earns his first All-Star MVP award.

2007

- After winning their first-ever Eastern Conference championship in franchise history, the Cavaliers and James both make their first NBA Finals appearance. They are defeated by the San Antonio Spurs in a four-game sweep.

- James's second son, Bryce, is born on June 14 amid the 2007 NBA Finals against the San Antonio Spurs.

- In one of his first forays into television, James hosts the thirty-third series premiere of *Saturday Night Live*.

2008

- James becomes the youngest player in NBA history to score 10,000 career points at 23 years and 59 days.

- James becomes the 2007–2008 NBA scoring champion after averaging 30 points per game that season.

- James joins the 2008 Olympic national team, nicknamed the "Redeem Team" after their poor performance during the 2004 Olympics. Team USA is undefeated and wins the gold medal in Beijing, the team's first gold since 2000.

2009

- James wins his first NBA MVP award for helping lead the Cavaliers to their franchise-best record of 66–16.

- James and the Cavaliers once again make it to the NBA Eastern Conference Finals. Though they are favored to win and make it to the NBA Finals, the Cavaliers lose to the Orlando Magic.

2010

- James wins his second consecutive NBA MVP award, becoming only the tenth player in NBA history to win back-to-back MVP awards.

- On July 8, James's controversial decision to leave the Cleveland Cavaliers—who hadn't won a championship during James's time on the team—for the Miami Heat is televised on ESPN in a special called *The Decision*. In the time after The Decision airs, James draws heavy criticism from fans and professionals in the industry alike. Fans take to burning his Cavaliers jersey and legendary players like Michael Jordan and Magic Johnson critique James for the move to Miami. Although *The Decision* raises over $3 million for charity, the backlash against James overshadows the ESPN special's philanthropic impact.

- Cleveland Cavaliers owner Dan Gilbert pens an open letter to Cavalier fans denouncing James, calling his actions "heartless" and a "cowardly betrayal" of the team and its fans.

- James is featured in the "People Who Mattered" section of *Time*'s Person of the Year issue, both for his consecutive MVP awards and impressive performance with the Cavaliers earlier that year and for his horrible ending with the Cavaliers before leaving the team for the Miami Heat.

2011

- James makes it to the NBA Finals with the Miami Heat. Despite forming a "Big 3" with fellow Heat players Dwyane Wade and Chris Bosh and being a favorite to win the Finals, James gives one of his lowest-scoring Finals performances, and the Heat loses in Game 6 to the Dallas Mavericks.

- The LeBron James Family Foundation launches the I PROMISE program, which today serves over 1,400 students across several Akron public schools by providing programs, resources, and mentorship to help them succeed in the classroom.

- Through the LeBron James Family Foundation, the new Wheels for Education program begins. With the support of various sponsors, laptops, school supplies, and bicycles are provided for each student in the program to help them stay in school and succeed all the way to graduation.

- James is inducted into St. Vincent–St. Mary's athletic hall of fame with several of his Fighting Irish teammates and friends.

2012

- James wins his first NBA championship with the Miami Heat and his first championship overall in his professional career, and earns both the regular-season and Finals MVP awards.

- James once again plays for Team USA in the London Olympics and helps lead the team to their second straight gold medal. He joins NBA legend Michael

Jordan as the only two players to win an NBA MVP award, an NBA championship, the NBA Finals MVP, and an Olympic gold medal all in the same year.

- James is named the *Sports Illustrated* Sportsman of the Year.

- James is chosen as the Male Athlete of the Year by USA Basketball for helping win the gold medal at the Olympics and leading the Miami Heat to win the NBA championship.

2013

- James becomes the youngest player in NBA history to score 20,000 points and surpass the 5,000-assist threshold.

- James marries his high school sweetheart Savannah James née Brinson on September 14.

- James wins his second NBA championship with the Heat, and his second championship overall, against the San Antonio Spurs. He once again earns MVP awards for both the Finals and the regular season, and he becomes the youngest player to win four regular-season MVP awards.

- The LeBron James Arena at St. Vincent–St. Mary High School, newly renovated due to a $1 million donation from James, opens.

2014

- The Miami Heat becomes the first team to win four consecutive Eastern Conference championships since the Boston Celtics during the 1984–1987 NBA seasons.

- James scores his career-best of 61 points in a single game against the Charlotte Bobcats, who become the Charlotte Hornets in the following season.

- After defeating the San Antonio Spurs the year previous, James plays against the Spurs once again in the Finals on the Heat's quest for a third Finals championship in a row. The Heat loses by a 4–1 margin.

- After his 2013–2014 season with the Heat, James becomes a free agent (a player who has no contract and so can sign with any team) once again.

- In an essay published in *Sports Illustrated,* four years after announcing his move to the Miami Heat, James announces his return home, re-signing with the Cleveland Cavaliers in hopes of fulfilling his mission of bringing a championship to his hometown. James writes, "what's most important for me is bringing one trophy back to Northeast Ohio. I always believed that I'd return to Cleveland and finish my career there." He closes his essay by telling Akron, Ohio, and Cavaliers fans, "I'm coming home." Compared to *The Decision,* his essay and announcement of returning to Cleveland are well-received by fans and met with excitement.

- James's daughter, Zhuri, is born on October 22.

2015

- In a partnership between the LeBron James Family Foundation and the University of Akron, eligible I PROMISE students are guaranteed a fully funded, four-year scholarship to the university to further pursue their education.

- James becomes the youngest player to score 25,000 career points at 30 years and 307 days, beating Kobe Bryant's previous record by over a year.

- James helps lead the Cavaliers to the NBA Finals against the Golden State Warriors. However, after losing Kevin Love and Kyrie Irving to injuries, the Cavaliers are bested 2–4. James is lauded for his performance during the Finals and for becoming the first player in NBA Finals history to lead both Finals teams in points, assists, and rebounds for the entire series.

2016

- The Cavaliers fire head coach David Blatt, with many noting the obvious tension between Blatt and James since the 2015 Finals. The Cavaliers' assistant coach Tyronn Lue steps in as the new head coach.

- James finally fulfills his promise to Cleveland and leads the Cleveland Cavaliers to win their first-ever NBA championship—and the city's first championship title in more than fifty years—beating the Golden State Warriors after coming back from a 3–1 deficit. The Cavaliers become the first team in NBA Finals history to recover from a 3–1 deficit and win. After their win, James emotionally tells Cavaliers fans, "Cleveland, this is for you."

His stunning performance secures his third Finals MVP award.

- The LeBron James Family Foundation establishes the I PROMISE Institute at the University of Akron as a resource center to help I PROMISE students thrive in college.

- James receives his second Sportsperson of the Year honor from *Sports Illustrated*.

2017

- James receives the J. Walter Kennedy Citizenship Award from the Professional Basketball Writers Association for the 2016–2017 season in recognition of his philanthropic work and service to the Akron community, and for his commitment to improving educational opportunities for the youth of Akron through the LeBron James Family Foundation.

- James also receives the NAACP Jackie Robinson Sports Award, becoming the first athlete in nearly two decades to receive the award after it was retired in 1999. This award is bestowed upon James for his "high achievement in athletics and [his] contributions in the pursuit of social justice, civil rights, and community involvement."

- The Cavaliers make it to the NBA Finals for their third straight season to face off against the Golden State Warriors for the third consecutive year. James becomes the first player in NBA history to record a triple-double average in the Finals, but the Cavaliers ultimately lose to the Warriors.

2018

- James sets an NBA record of scoring double digits in 867 consecutive games.

- The Cavaliers make it to their fourth Finals in a row—and James's eighth consecutive championship appearance—once again facing the Golden State Warriors, but are defeated in overtime for Game 1. As a result of the loss, James punches his hand into a whiteboard in the locker room, sustaining a severe bone contusion (bone bruise). He continues to play in the next three games of the Finals, but his injury affects his performance. The Cavaliers are swept in four games, the first Finals sweep since 2007 when the LeBron-led Cavaliers were swept by the San Antonio Spurs.

- In July, James officially signs with the Los Angeles Lakers. The announcement is met with a more positive reaction compared to his previous move to the Miami Heat.

- The LeBron James Family Foundation's I PROMISE School, a public elementary school devoted to helping struggling students stay in school, officially opens in James's hometown of Akron, Ohio, welcoming 240 students on the first day of school.

- *The Shop: Uninterrupted*, a talk show starring James and his lifelong friend and business partner Maverick Carter, premieres on HBO. The show features celebrity guests as they have honest conversations and discussions with James and Carter inside a U.S. barbershop.

- On Christmas Day, James and the Lakers face the Golden State Warriors and win by a large margin. However,

James sustains a groin injury, the first major injury of his career, causing him to miss seventeen consecutive games.

2019

- As a result of James's groin injury, James is eventually ruled out for the remainder of the 2018–2019 season, only playing a total of fifty-five games for the season. The Lakers end up failing to make it to the playoffs for the sixth season in a row, marking the first time James is absent from the playoffs since the 2004–2005 season. This also breaks James's eight-year streak of appearing in every NBA Finals since 2011.

- James is named by *Time* as one of the 100 most influential people in the world for the fourth time, after previously making the list in 2005, 2013, and 2017.

- The LeBron James Family Foundation announces the I PROMISE Village, which provides I PROMISE students and their families a safe place to stay if they are experiencing homelessness, domestic violence, and other extreme circumstances.

2020

- Kent State University joins the University of Akron in offering I PROMISE students free tuition to pursue their degrees.

- With the help of the LeBron James Family Foundation, James hosts a virtual graduation for the Class of 2020, as graduation ceremonies are canceled and moved online due to the ongoing COVID-19 pandemic. The graduation is broadcast on major TV networks and streamed on various social media platforms, with appearances from celebrity guests such as Barack Obama, Megan Rapinoe, and Zendaya to celebrate the graduating class and honor their achievements amid an unconventional year.

- James cofounds SpringHill Company, an entertainment development and production company, with his business partner Maverick Carter. Named for the apartment complex in Akron, Ohio, where James moved in sixth grade, the company unites three earlier companies James and Carter had founded together and seeks to empower and elevate diverse creators and their communities.

- Despite playing in an abbreviated season due to the COVID-19 pandemic, James leads the Lakers to their first Pacific Division title since 2012, their first top seed in the Western Conference playoffs since the 2009–2010 season, and ultimately victory in the NBA Finals against his former team, the Miami Heat. He secures his fourth championship and fourth Finals MVP award, becoming the second-oldest player in the league's history to win the award and the only player in the NBA's history to win the award in three different franchises.

- James becomes the first athlete to be named the *Sports Illustrated* Sportsperson of the Year three times, having previously won the award in 2012 and 2016.

- James receives the 2020 *Sports Illustrated* Muhammad Ali Legacy Award for his social activism in the midst of COVID-19, police brutality, and voter suppression. Ali's widow, Lonnie Ali, says James "continues to embody Muhammad's principles and core beliefs, using his celebrity platform to champion social justice and political causes that uplift all people."

- James is named *Time*'s Athlete of the Year for founding the nonprofit More Than a Vote in response to the racial injustice and police brutality that mark much of the year to spur voters, especially Black voters, to vote in the 2020 presidential election despite historic voter suppression efforts. James recruits prominent athletes from all over the sports world to take part in the organization, vote, and urge fans to follow in their footsteps. More Than a Vote also seeks to open sports arenas as polling places on Election Day and to enlist younger people to replace older poll workers due to health concerns from the COVID-19 pandemic. He is heralded for being one of the first prominent sports figures to bridge the gap between commercial appeal and political duty, something many athletes had been hesitant to do for fear of tarnishing their image.

- On his thirty-sixth birthday, James becomes the first player in NBA history to score double-digit points in 1,000 consecutive games.

2021

- James sustains a high ankle sprain during a game against the Atlanta Hawks. The Lakers announce that James will be out indefinitely for the rest of the season. In total, James misses twenty-six games—the highest number of absences in a season throughout his career. James and the Lakers later make it to the NBA playoffs, but due to numerous player injuries and James still recovering from his own injury, the Lakers lose against the Phoenix

Suns. This marks the first time James has lost in the first round of the playoffs.

- James receives the President's Award at the 52nd annual NAACP Image Awards for his "leadership, sportsmanship, and commitment to social justice," recognizing "his work both on and off the court," including the work he has done through the LeBron James Family Foundation and More Than a Vote.

- James stars in *Space Jam: A New Legacy*, a sequel/reboot of the original *Space Jam* (1996) that starred NBA legend Michael Jordan.

- James is selected to the NBA 75th Anniversary Team, an honor that names the greatest players in league history. James is one of eleven players chosen who are still active in the 2021–2022 season and one of four players playing for the Los Angeles Lakers.

2022

- James becomes the only player in NBA history to record at least 10,000 points, 10,000 rebounds, and 10,000 assists.

- In April, the Lakers announce that due to a left ankle injury sustained during a game against the New Orleans Pelicans, James will sit out for the remainder of the 2021–2022 season in order to recover.

- *Forbes* declares James to be a billionaire. He is the first NBA player to become a billionaire while still actively playing.

- James re-signs with the Lakers on a two-year, $97.1 million contract, making him the highest-paid athlete in NBA history.

- James is featured alongside his sons on the cover of *Sports Illustrated*, entitled "The Chosen Sons," an echo of James's first appearance on the magazine cover titled "The Chosen One" twenty years earlier.

- James voices his desire to play professional basketball beside his sons Bronny, who will be eligible for the draft in 2024, and Bryce, who will be eligible in 2027.

2023

- James is selected to play at the 2023 NBA All-Star Game, tying with former Laker Kareem Abdul-Jabbar for the most All-Star selections at nineteen. The 2023 game marks James's nineteenth consecutive All-Star appearance, and also sets a record for most All-Star games played, breaking Kareem Abdul-Jabbar's former record of eighteen.

- On January 31, James breaks into the top five and moves up to fourth place on the NBA career assists list with a total of 10,338 assists.

- On February 7, James becomes the leading scorer in all of the NBA, surpassing former Laker Kareem Abdul-Jabbar's nearly thirty-nine-year-old record and scoring his 38,388th career point.

- The Lakers defeat the Golden State Warriors, the defending 2022 NBA champions, to secure their place in the 2023 Western Conference Finals. James wins his forty-first playoff series, the most in NBA history.

- James and the Lakers make it to the Conference Finals but are swept by the Denver Nuggets in four games. This is the first time James loses in the Conference Finals since 2009 with the Cavaliers against the Orlando Magic.

Glossary

ACCOUNTABLE	(adj.): responsible for
ADVERSITY	(noun): a state of hardship or difficulty
APEX	(noun): the highest point
ASPIRATION	(noun): desire for success and achievement
ASSISTS	(noun): the action of a player helping their teammate score
COALITION	(noun): a group of people working toward a common goal
COMPLACENCY	(noun): the state of being overly comfortable or satisfied with one's own performance
CRITIQUE	(verb): criticize
DYNAMIC	(adj.): often changing
FIRST-GENERATION	(adj.): the first member of a family to reach a cerwtain milestone
FRANCHISE	(noun): a team and its entire organization, often tied to its historical significance
FRUITION	(noun): coming to be, being realized
GRATIFYING	(adj.): pleasing, rewarding
HUMBLED	(verb): reminded of one's own shortcomings; (adj.): not boastful or full of oneself
INDEBTED	(adj.): owing gratitude to
INSTILL	(verb): teach, little by little

LEGACY	(noun): what someone leaves behind, what people remember of them
LIKENESS	(noun): picture of a person
LONGEVITY	(noun): the ability to exist or last for a long time
MANTRA	(noun): a strong personal belief
MISOGYNY	(noun): prejudice against women
PREDICATED	(verb): founded or based on
RESPECTIVE	(adj.): particular, individual
SYSTEMIC	(adj.): dependent on social, economic, or political parts of a society such that they cannot be separated from it
THRESHOLD	(noun): a boundary or point at which something will happen
ULTIMATELY	(adv.): in the end, eventually
UNDERPRIVI-LEGED	(adj.): not provided the same social or economic rights as other members of a society
VISIONARY	(noun): someone who has ideas for the future

Additional Resources

Alexander, Kwame (author) and Dawud Anyabwile (illustrator). *The Crossover*. Clarion, 2014.
- This coming-of-age story about a middle school basketball player trying to figure life out is also available as a graphic novel (Clarion, 2019).

Benedict, Jeff. *LeBron*. Simon & Schuster, 2023.
- Based on hundreds of interviews and three years of research, biographer Jeff Benedict tells LeBron James's story of rocketing from humble beginnings to cultural icon status.

Brundage, Vernon Jr. *Shoot Your Shot: A Sport-Inspired Guide to Living Your Best Life*. 2018.
- Learn the steps and principles that the greatest basketball players of all time have used to achieve success and get motivated to accomplish your own dreams.

Geoffreys, Clayton. *LeBron James: The Inspiring Story of One of Basketball's Greatest Players*. 2023.
- This brief biography explores the highlights of LeBron James's life and greatest triumphs.

Grundy, Pamela and Susan Shackelford. *Shattering The Glass: The Remarkable History of Women's Basketball*. The New Press, 2005.
- This history of women's basketball highlights the struggles and triumphs of the sport's female players from the time it was invented through the explosion of the WNBA's popularity.

James, LeBron and Buzz Bissinger. *Shooting Stars*. Penguin, 2009.

- Journalist Buzz Bissinger helps LeBron James tell the story of his young teammates in Akron, Ohio, who bonded over their love of basketball and stuck together all the way to the national championship during their senior year of high school.

Johnson, Mike. *Inspirational Basketball Stories for Young Readers*. Curious Press, 2023.

- Get inspired by these twelve true stories about basketball players who beat the odds on and off the court.

More Than a Game. Lionsgate, 2008.

- This documentary follows LeBron James and his Akron, Ohio, teammates on their journey from unknown to basketball superstardom.

Pappas, Elizabeth and Emily Feng (editors). *LeBron James: In His Own Words*. Agate Publishing, 2024.

- This is the full-length title from which this Young Readers edition was created. The full-length version includes additional quotations from LeBron James.

Windhorst, Brian and Dave McMenamin. *Return of the King: LeBron James, the Cleveland Cavaliers and the Greatest Comeback in NBA History*. Grand Central, 2018.

- A deep dive into LeBron James's return to Cleveland, from the secret meetings to the heart-stopping Game 7 when the Cavs won the 2016 NBA title.

www.basketball-reference.com.

- Access basketball statistics, scores, and history for every player and team in both the NBA and the WNBA.

Acknowledgments

We would like to thank Henry Begler, Johnna Caboz, Kelsey Dame, Madelyn Erickson, Marta Evans, Paige Gilberg, Mira Green, Eva Lopez, Julia Poetzinger, Emma Ramirez, Erin Rosenberg, Madiha Saber, Suzanne Sonnier, and Connor White for their invaluable contributions to the preparation of this manuscript.